Daz Activity Book

This Book Belongs To

Name:

Address:

Phone Number:

Email:

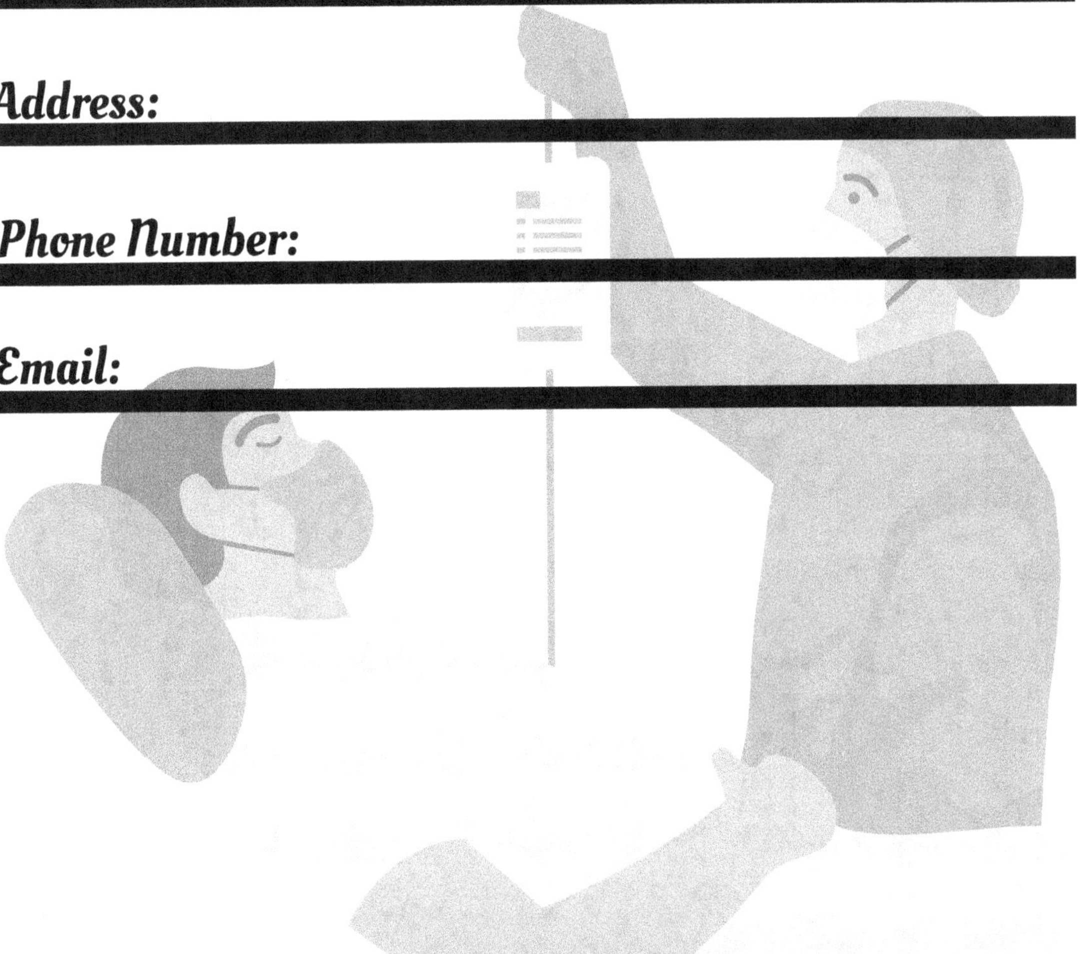

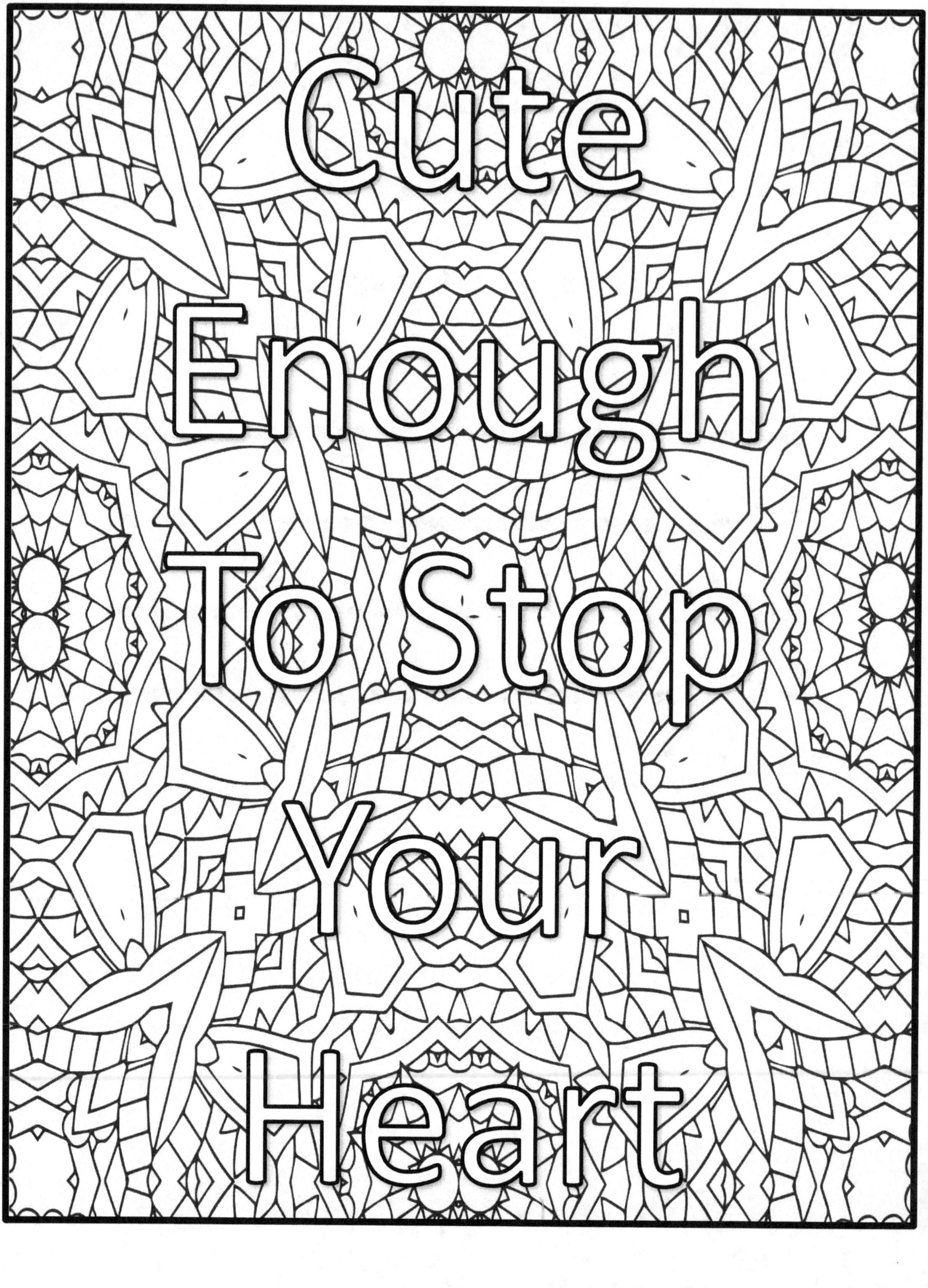
Cute
Enough
To Stop
Your
Heart

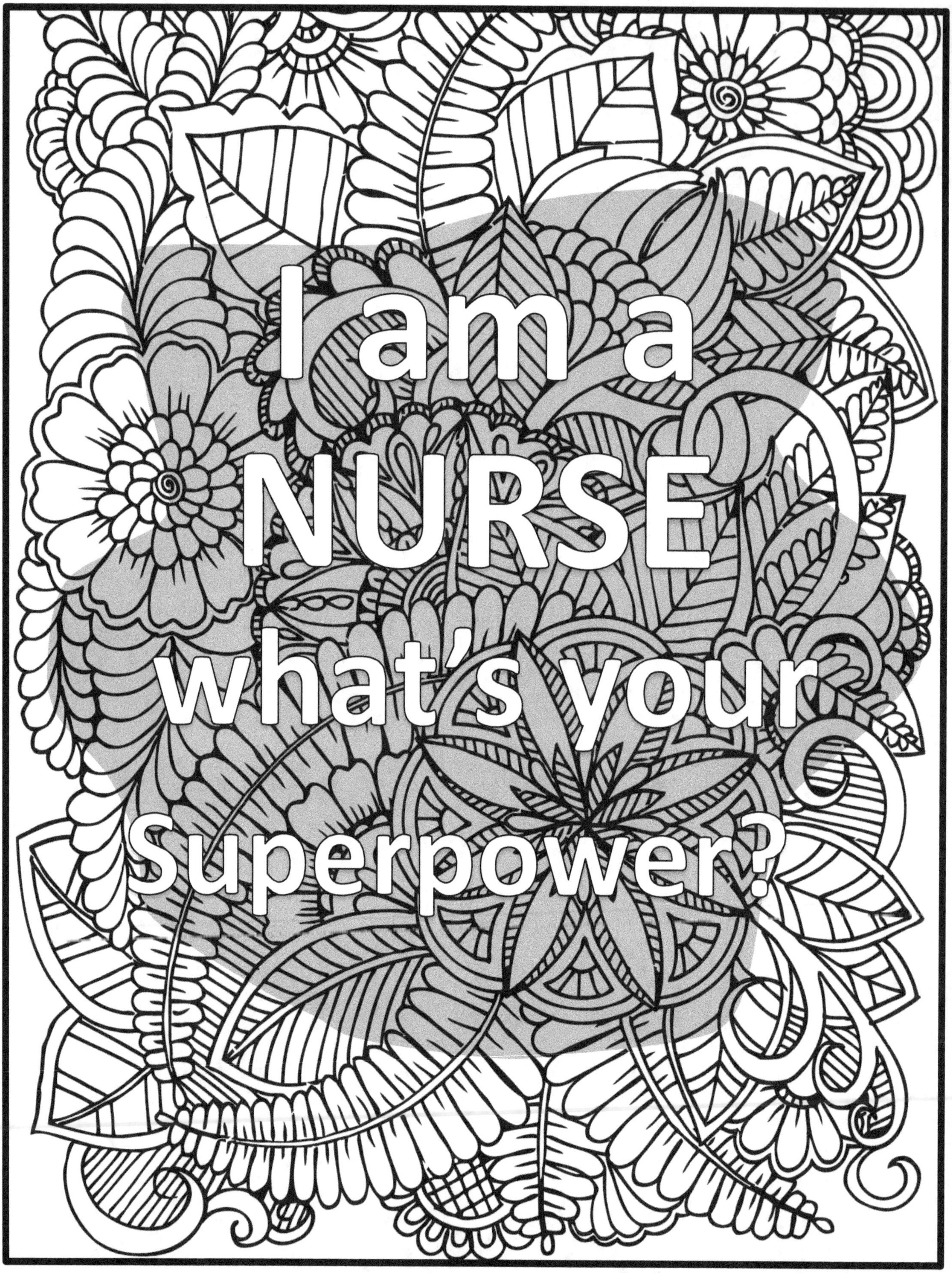
I am a
NURSE
what's your
Superpower?

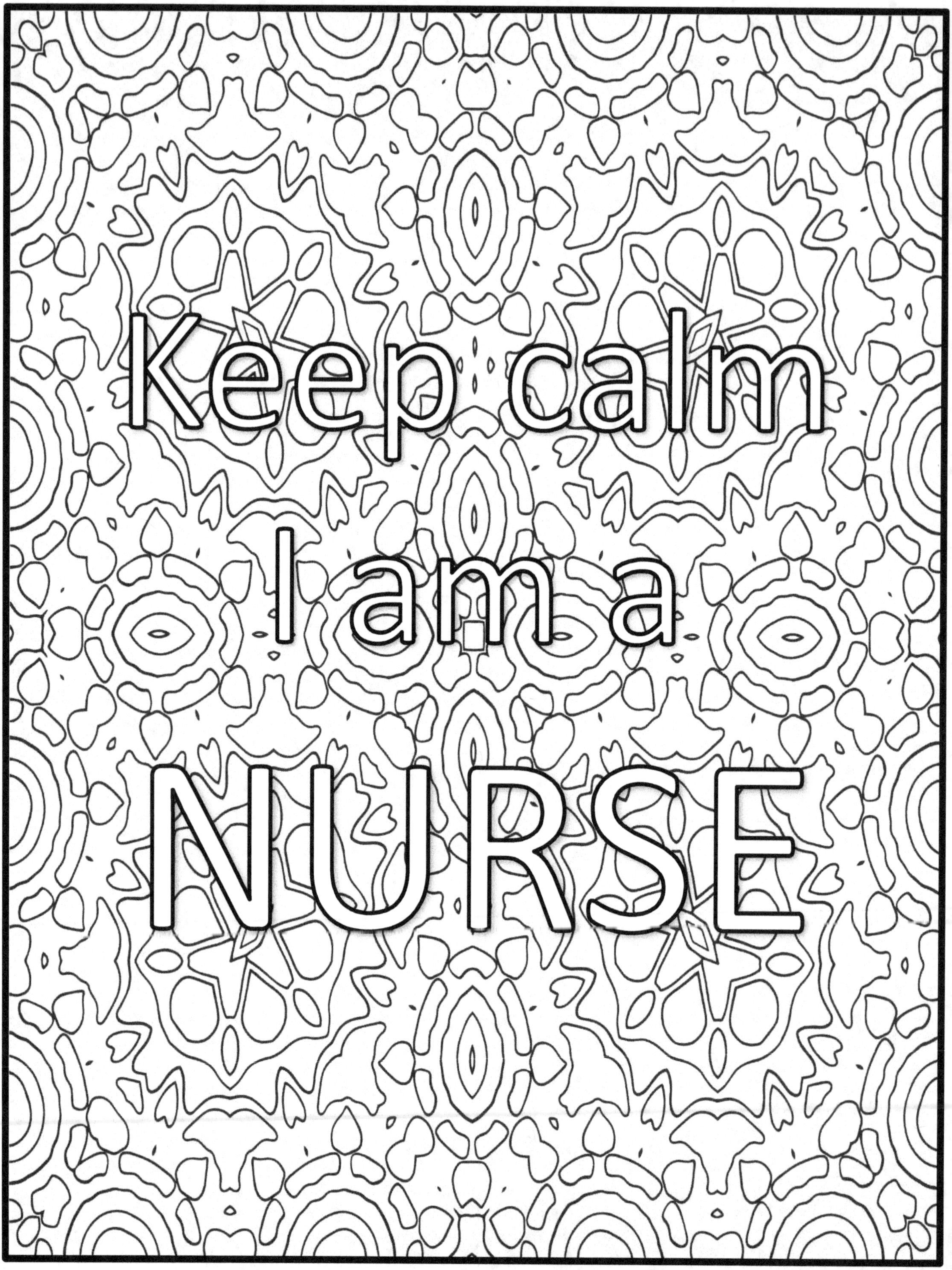
Keep calm
I am a
NURSE

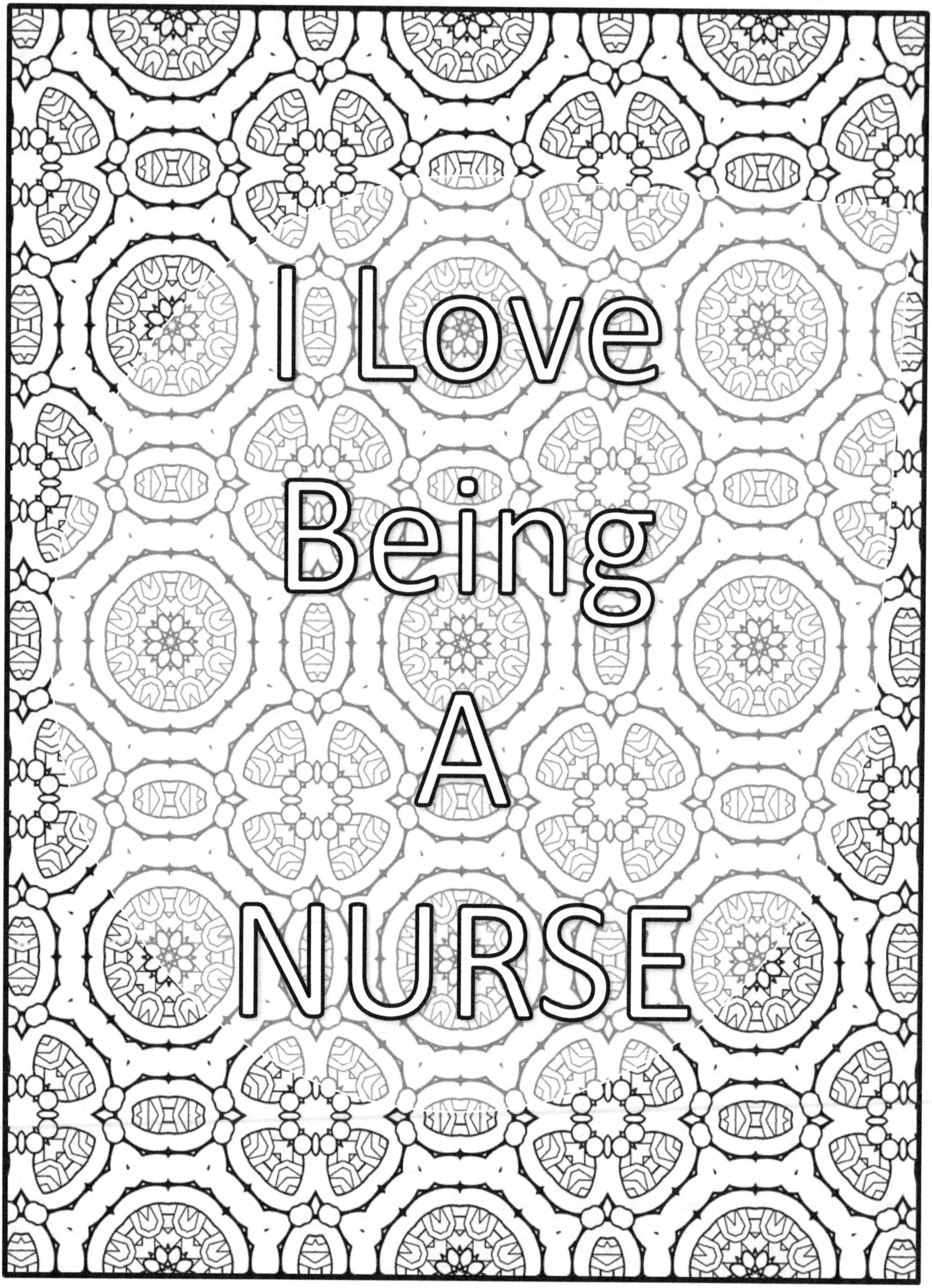
I Love
Being
A
NURSE

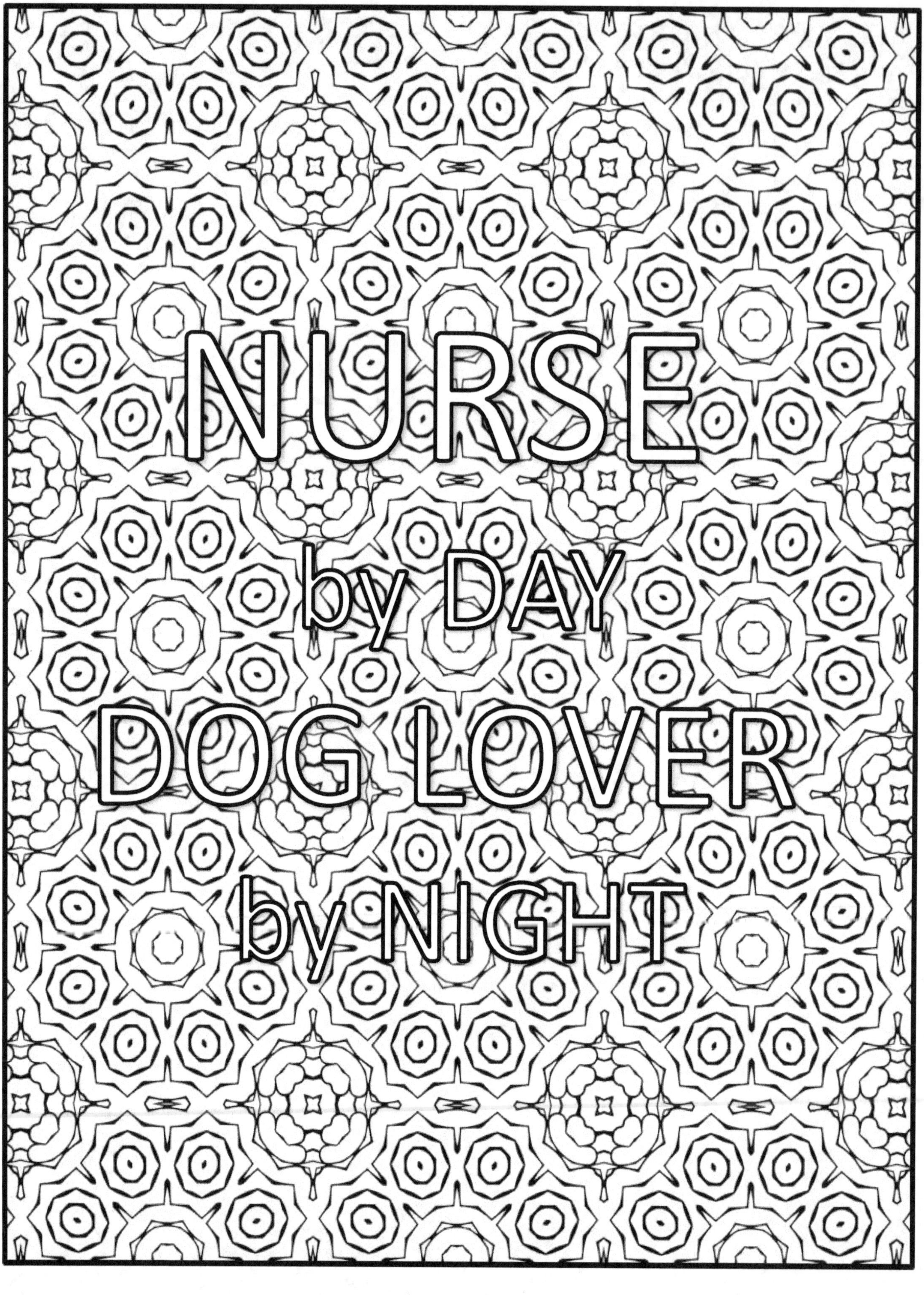
NURSE
by DAY
DOG LOVER
by NIGHT

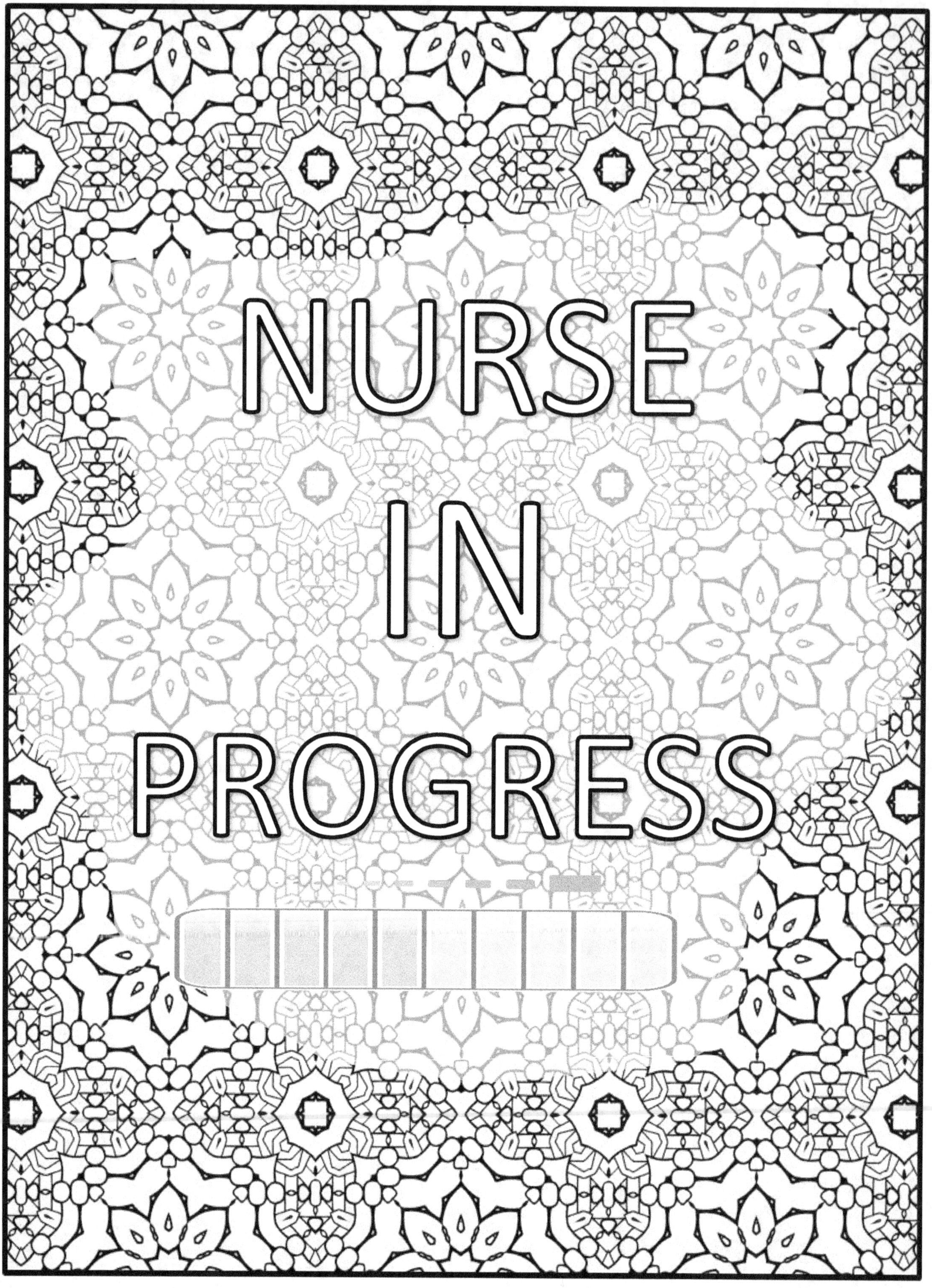
NURSE
IN
PROGRESS

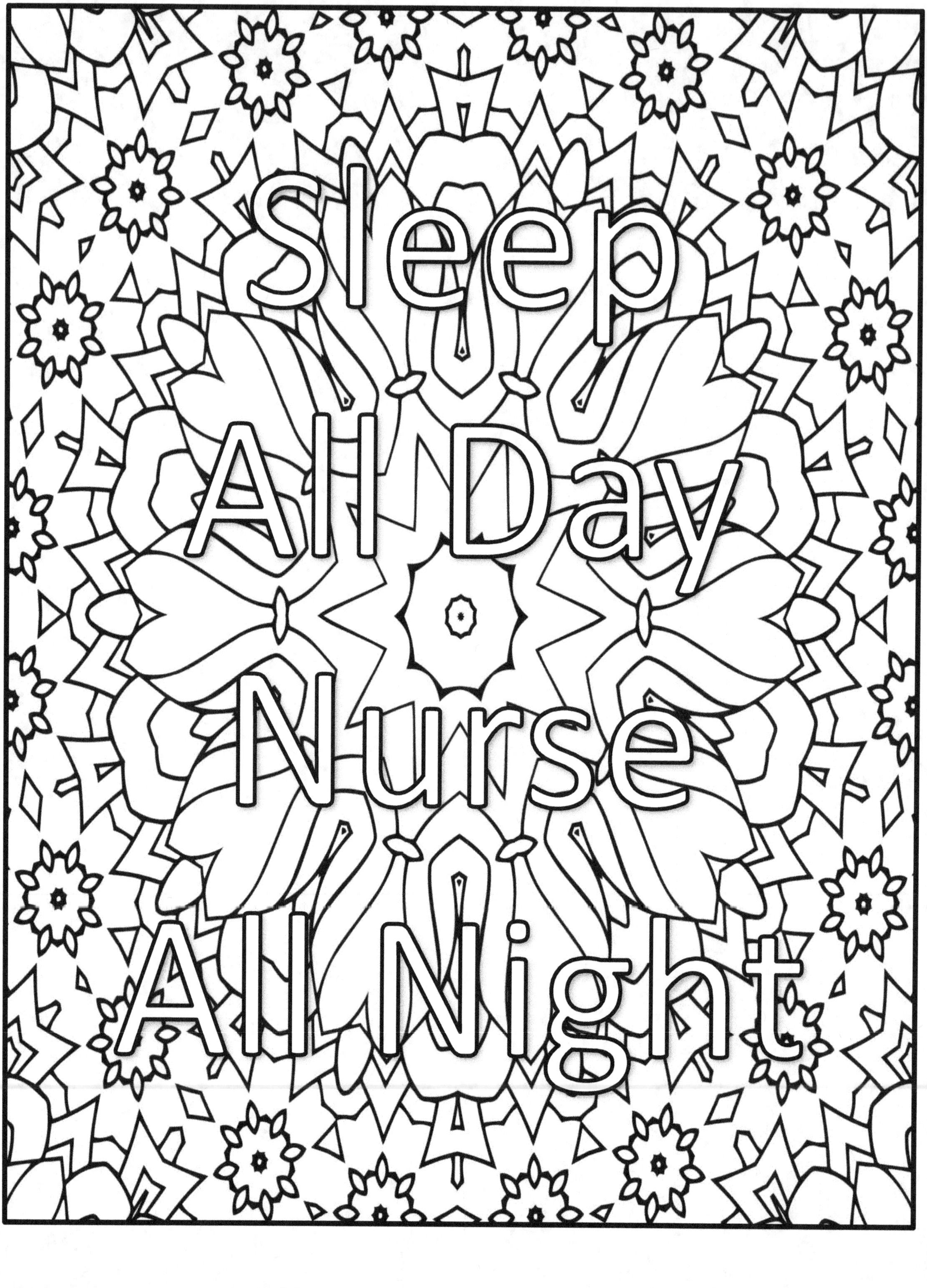
Sleep
All Day
Nurse
All Night

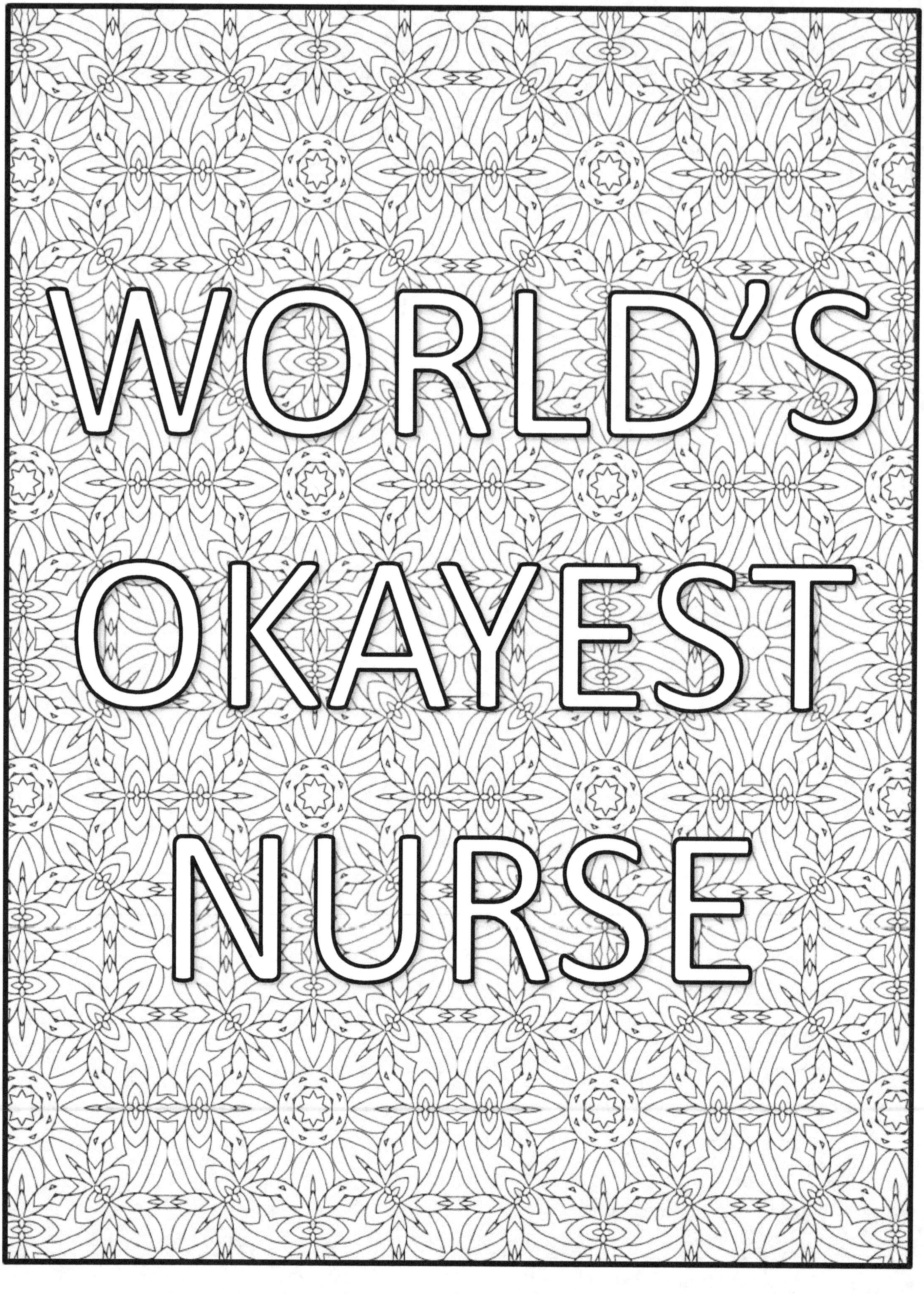
WORLD'S
OKAYEST
NURSE

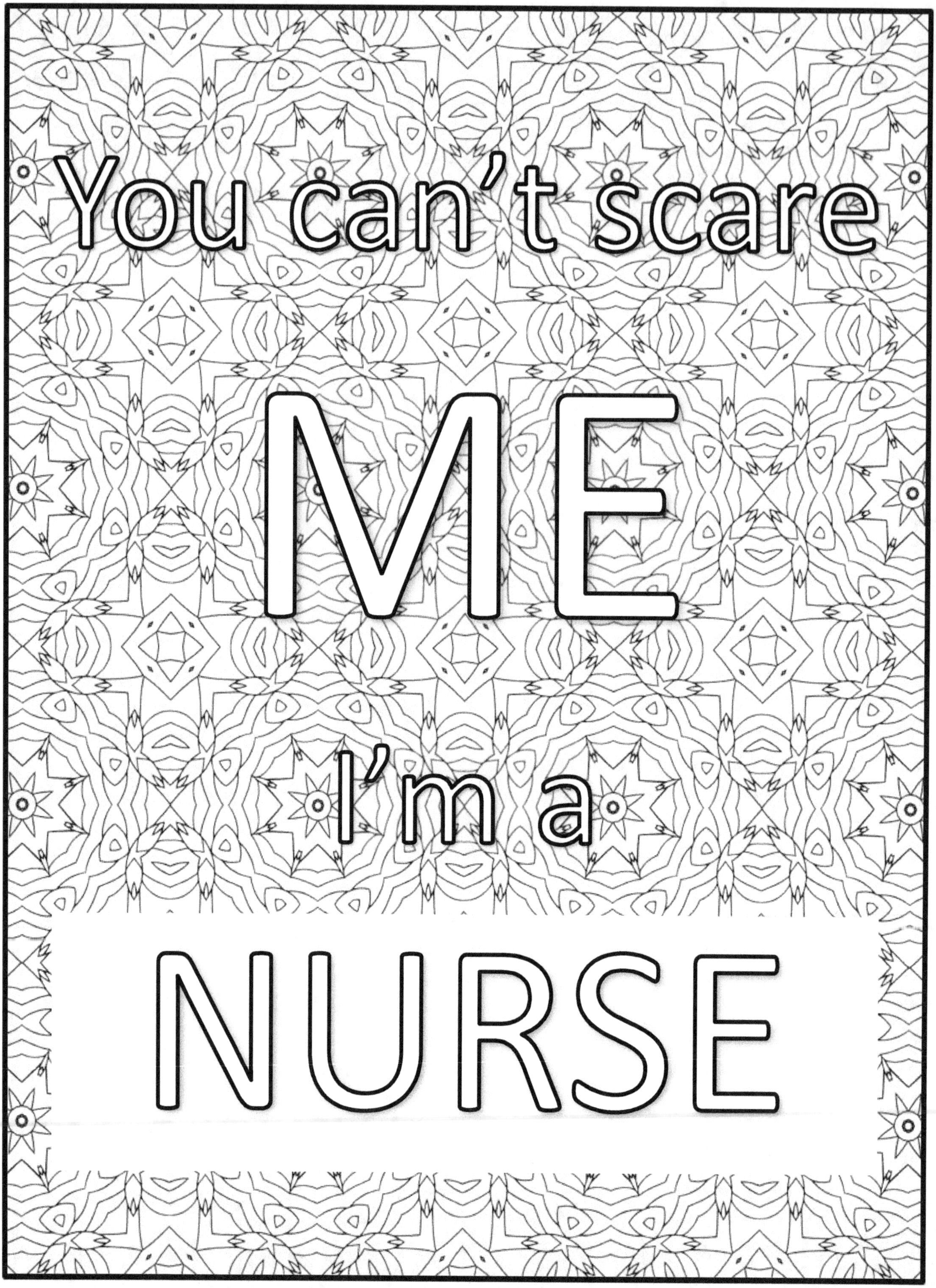
You can't scare
ME
I'm a
NURSE

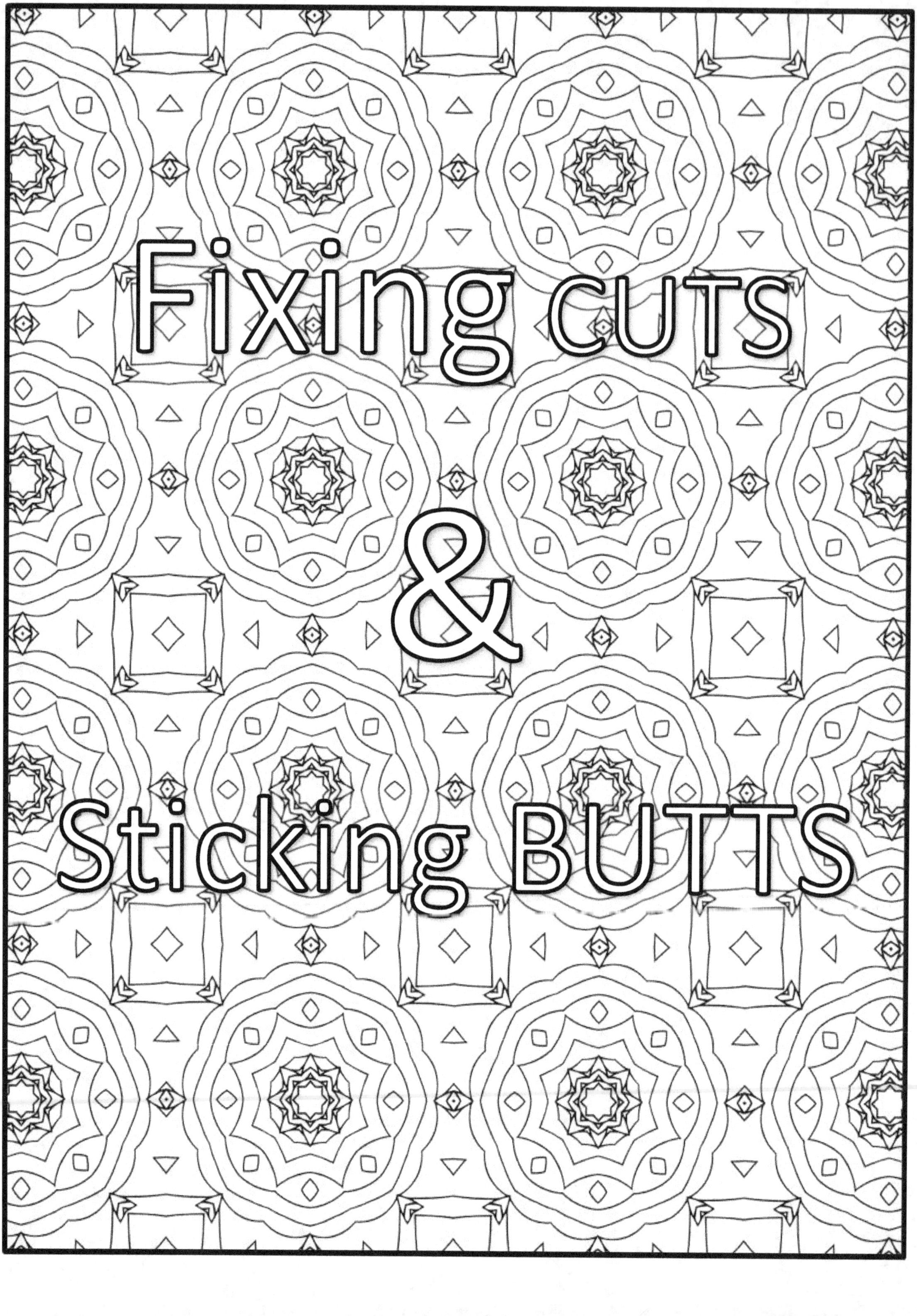
Fixing cuts
&
Sticking BUTTS

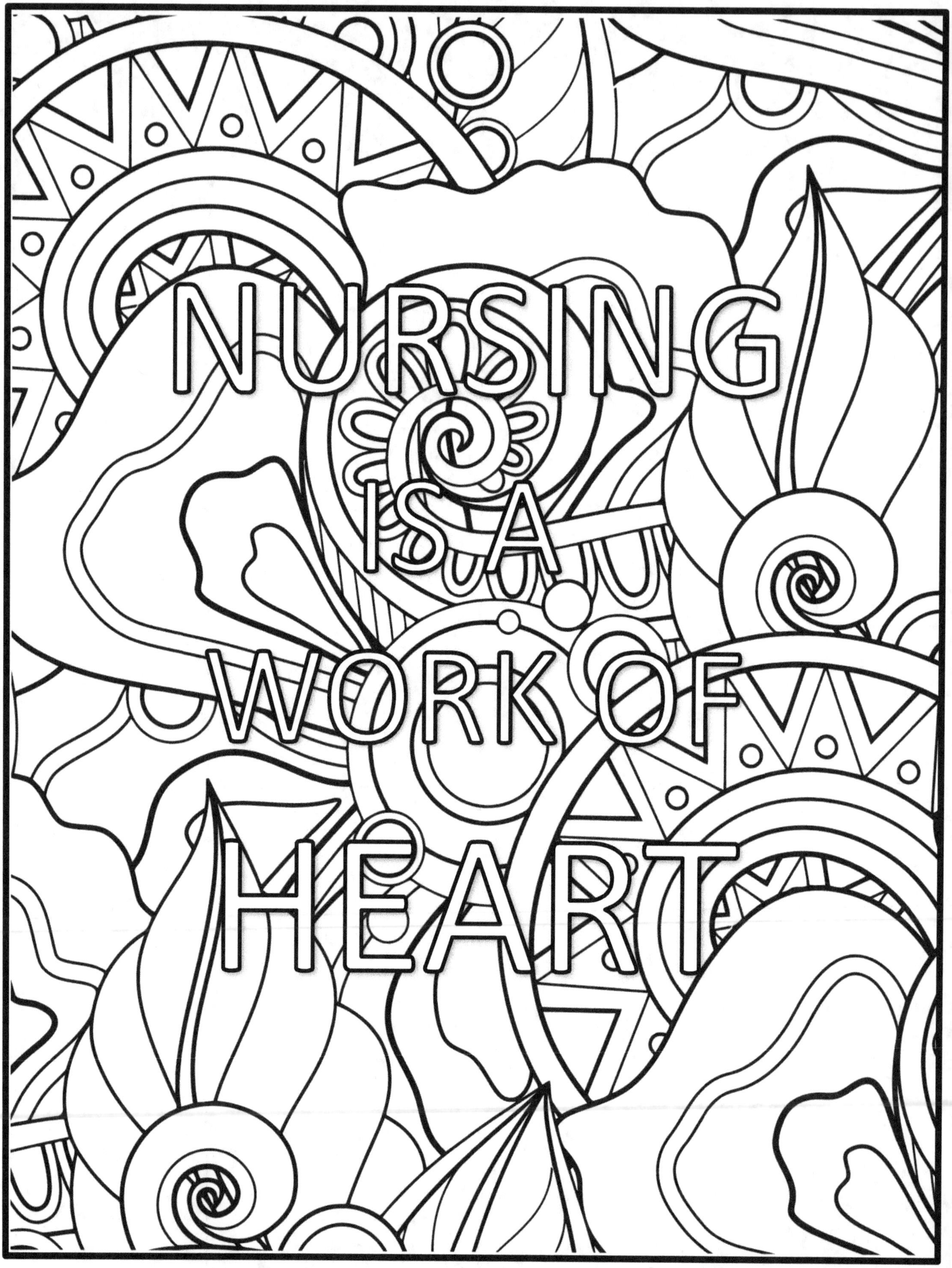
NURSING
IS A
WORK OF
HEART

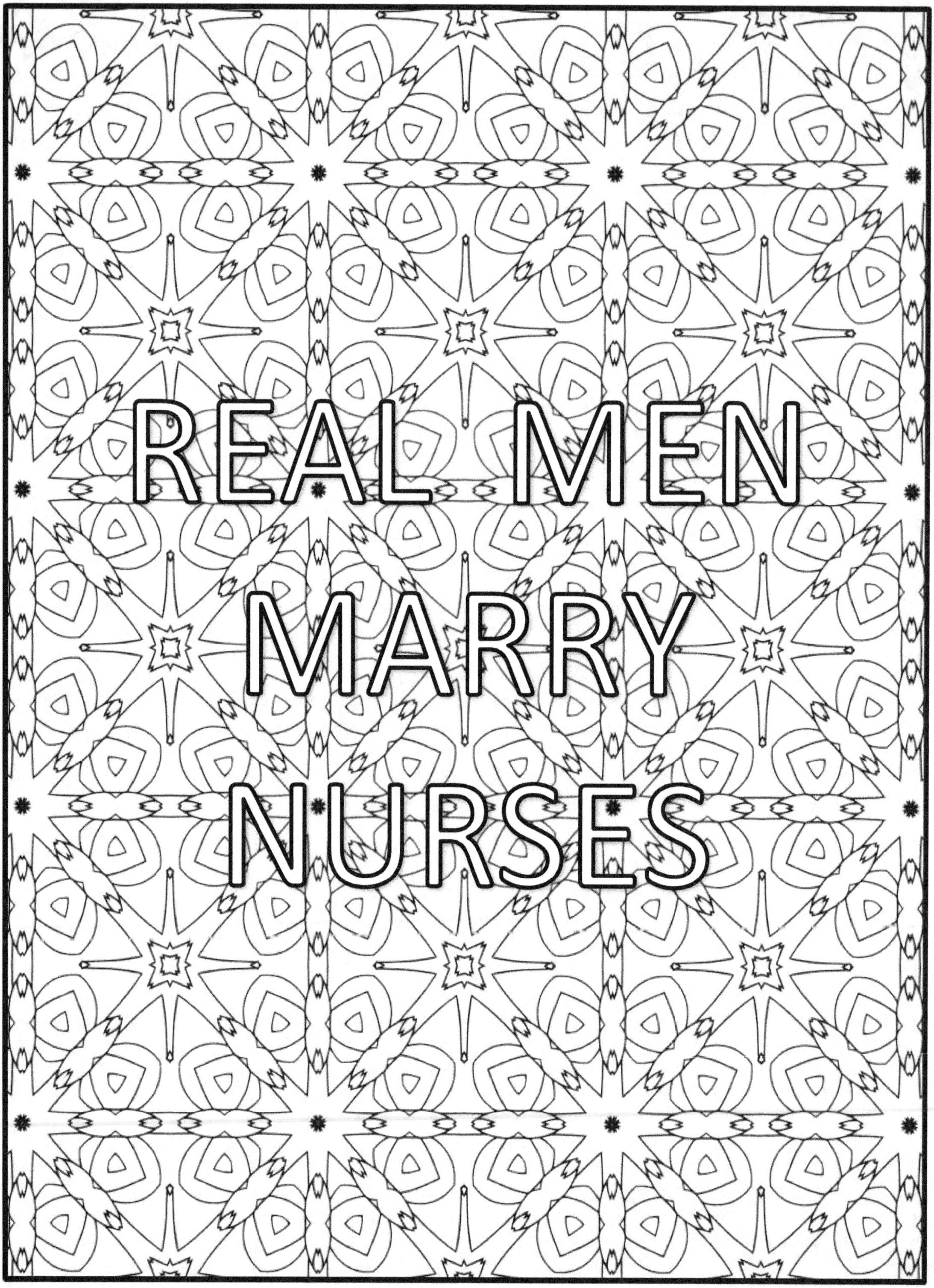
REAL MEN
MARRY
NURSES

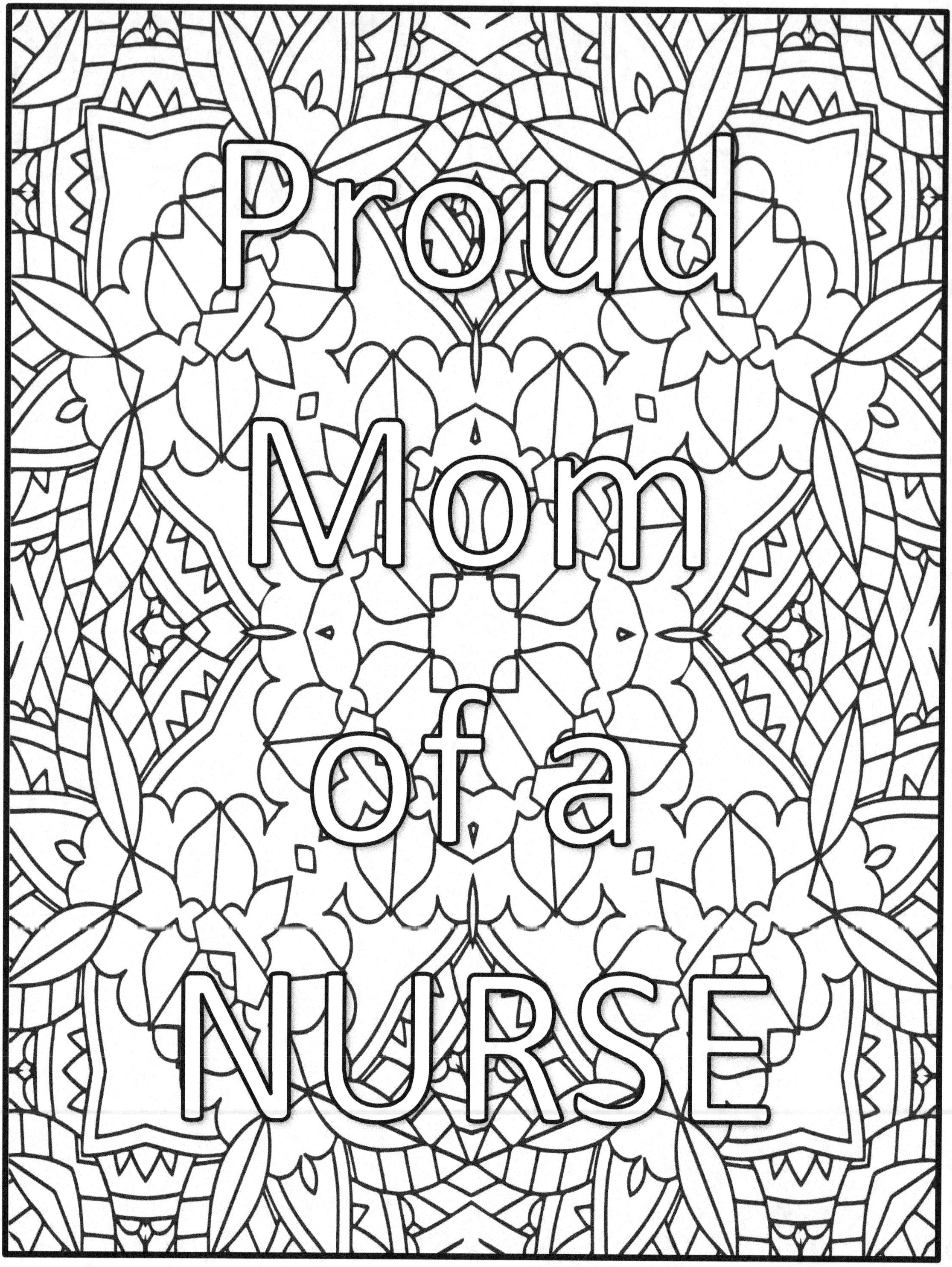
Proud
Mom
of a
NURSE

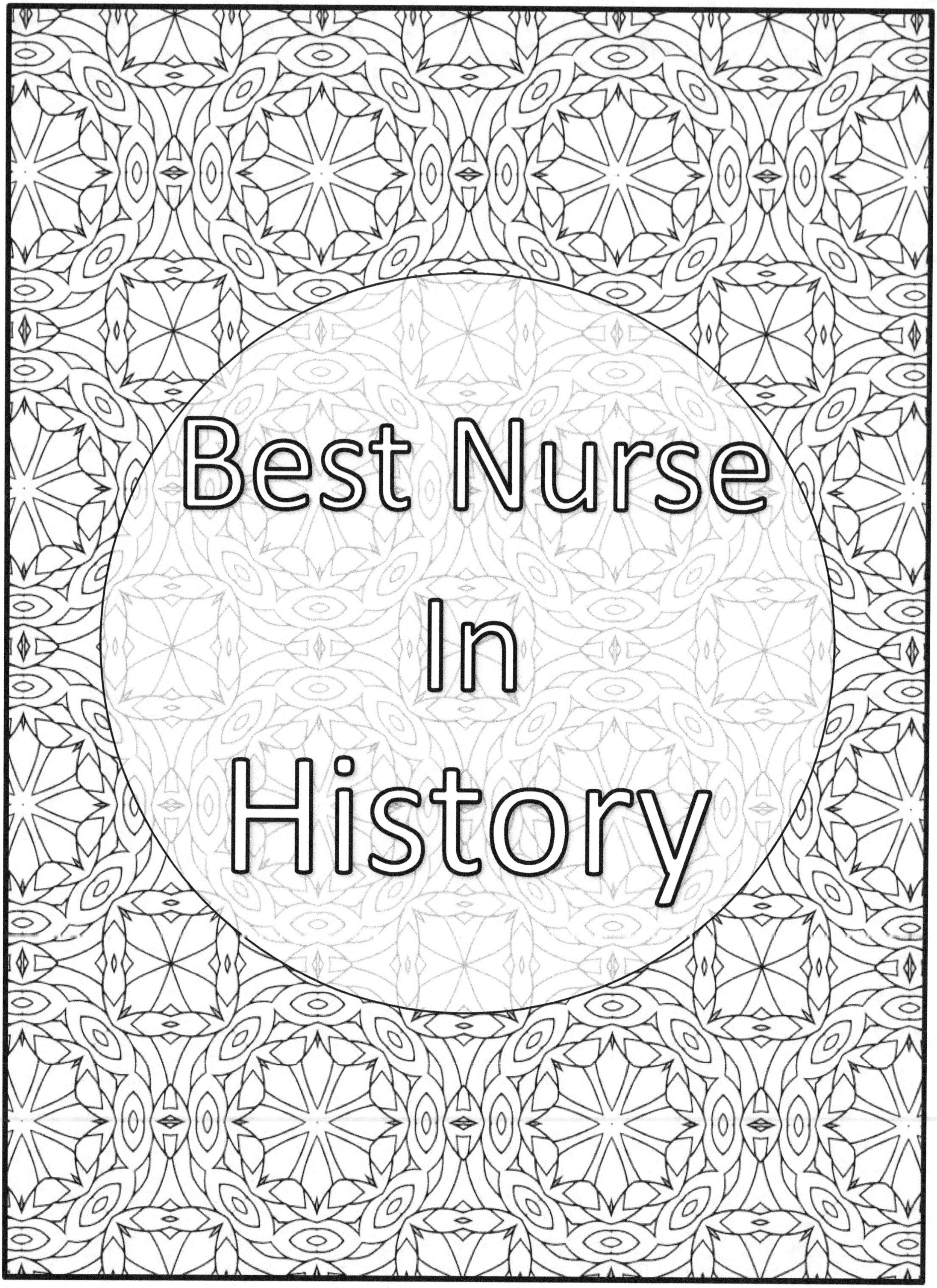
Best Nurse
In
History

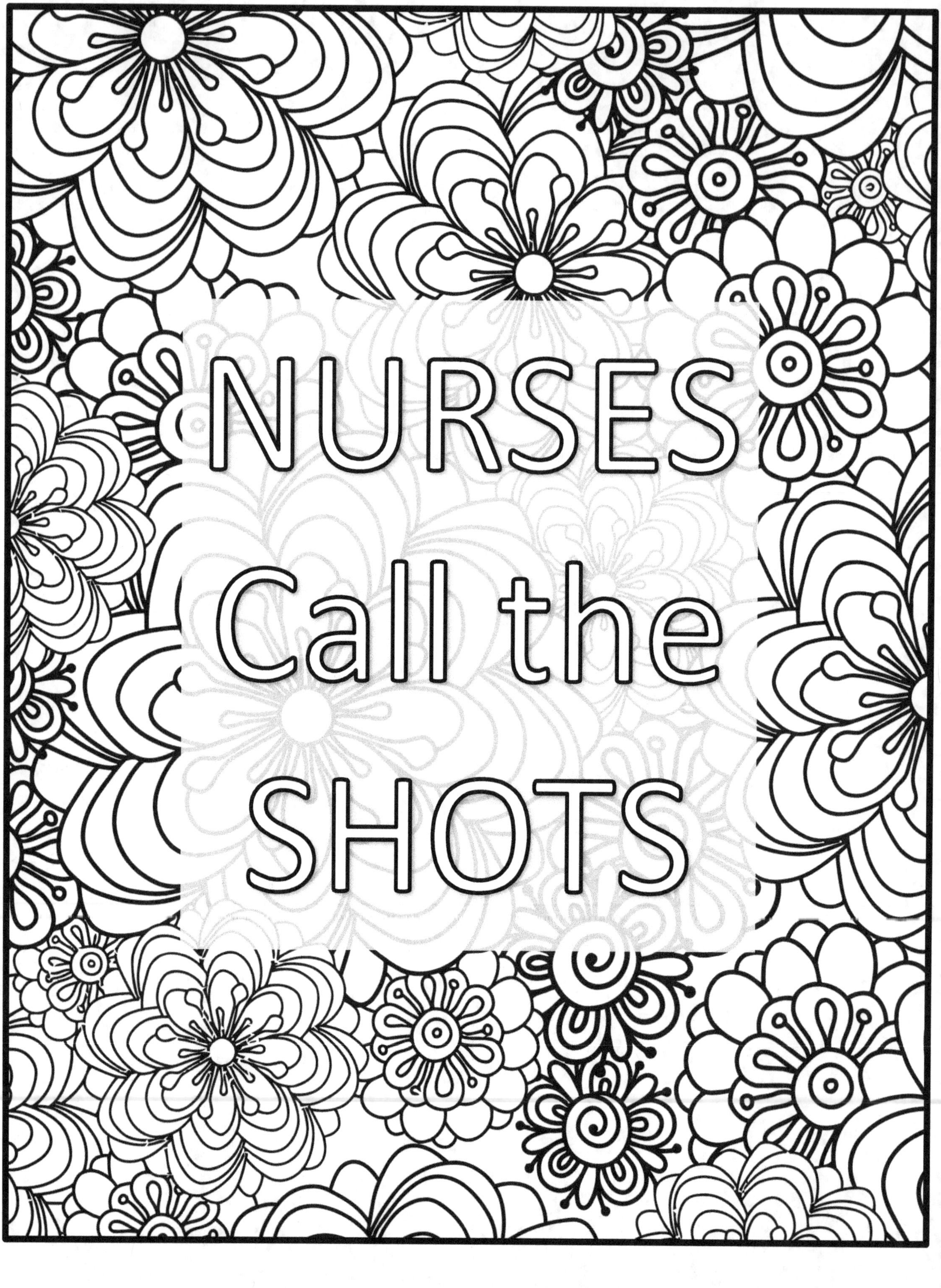
NURSES
Call the
SHOTS

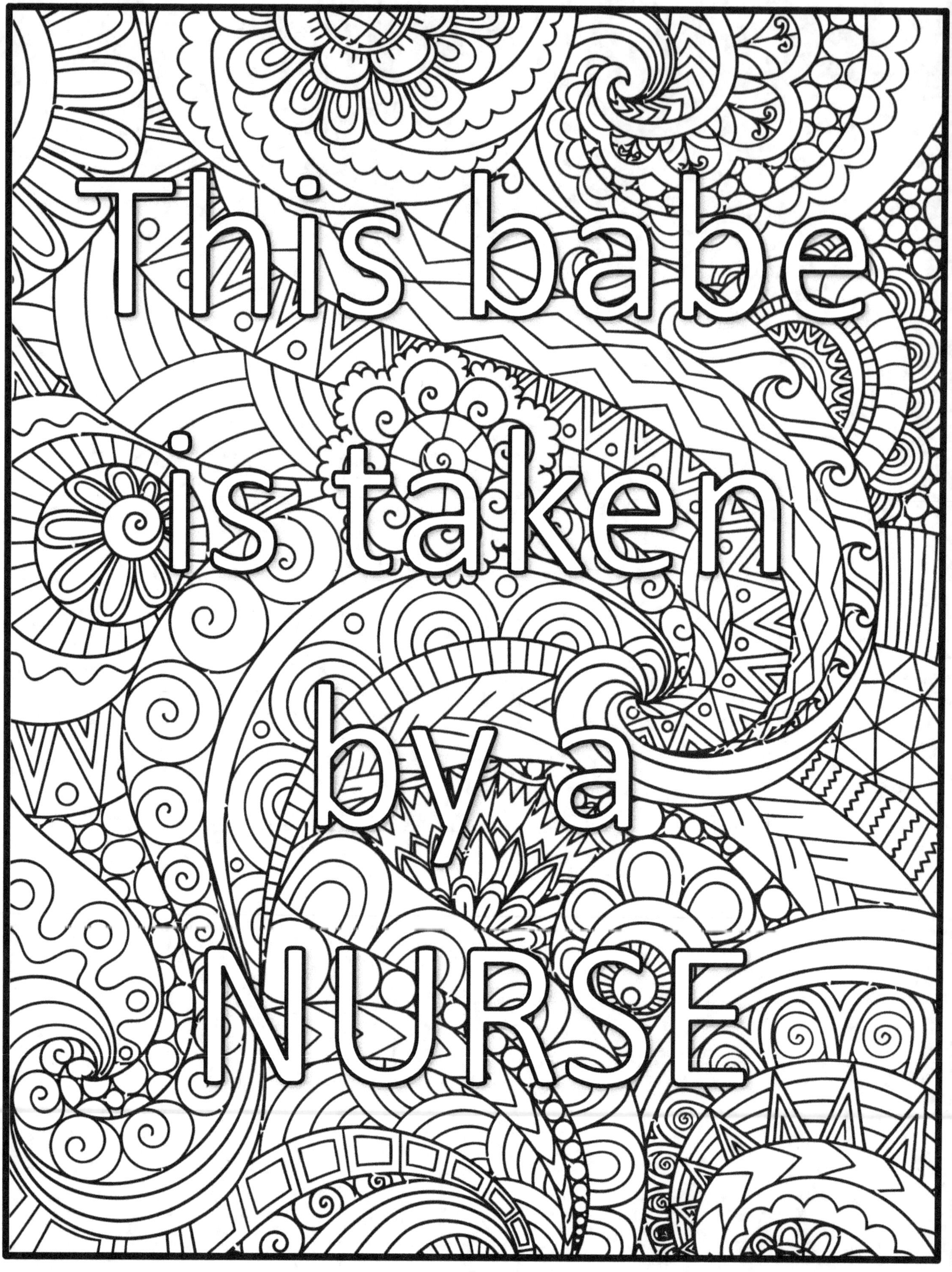
This babe
is taken
by a
NURSE

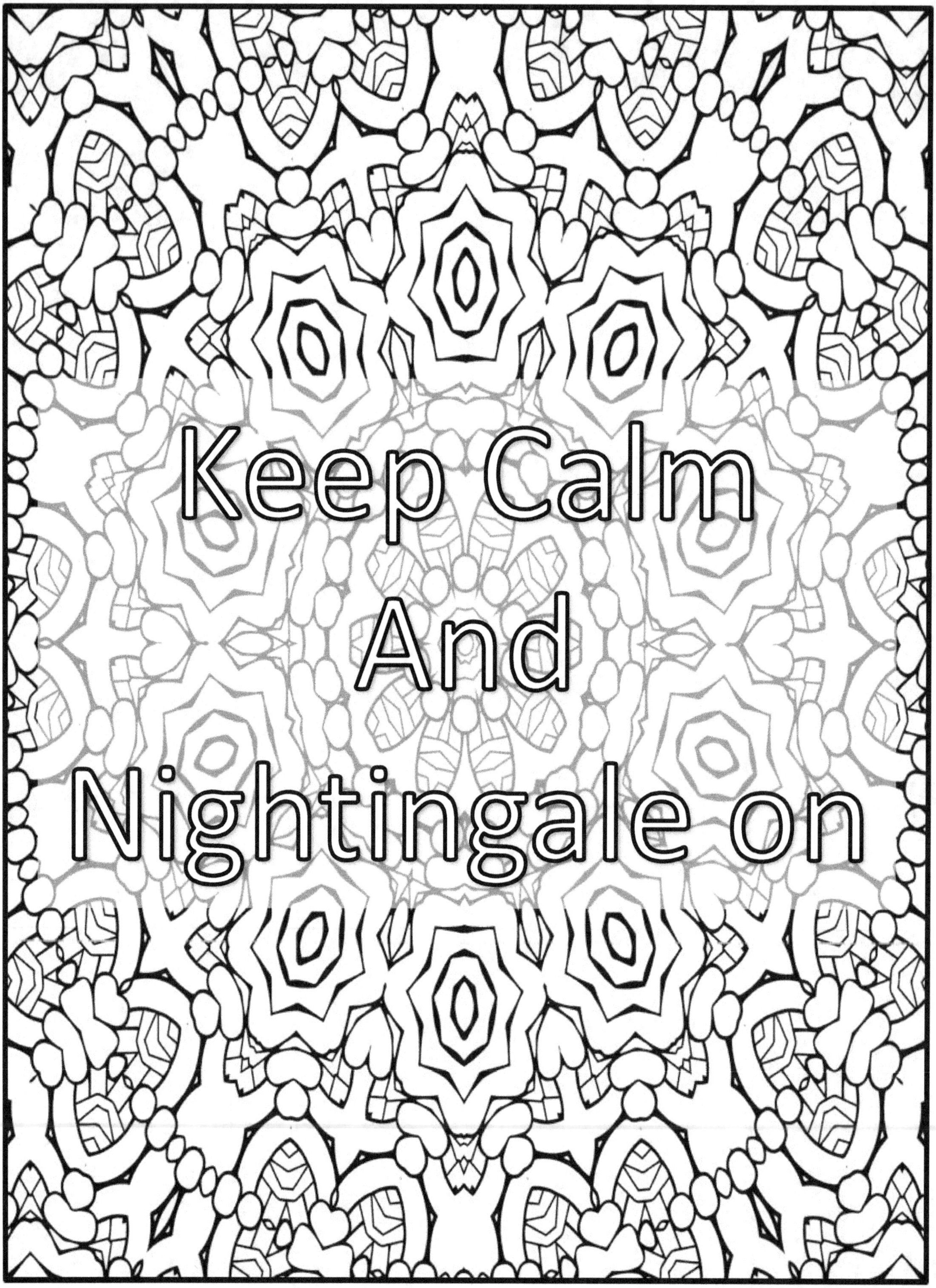
Keep Calm
And
Nightingale on

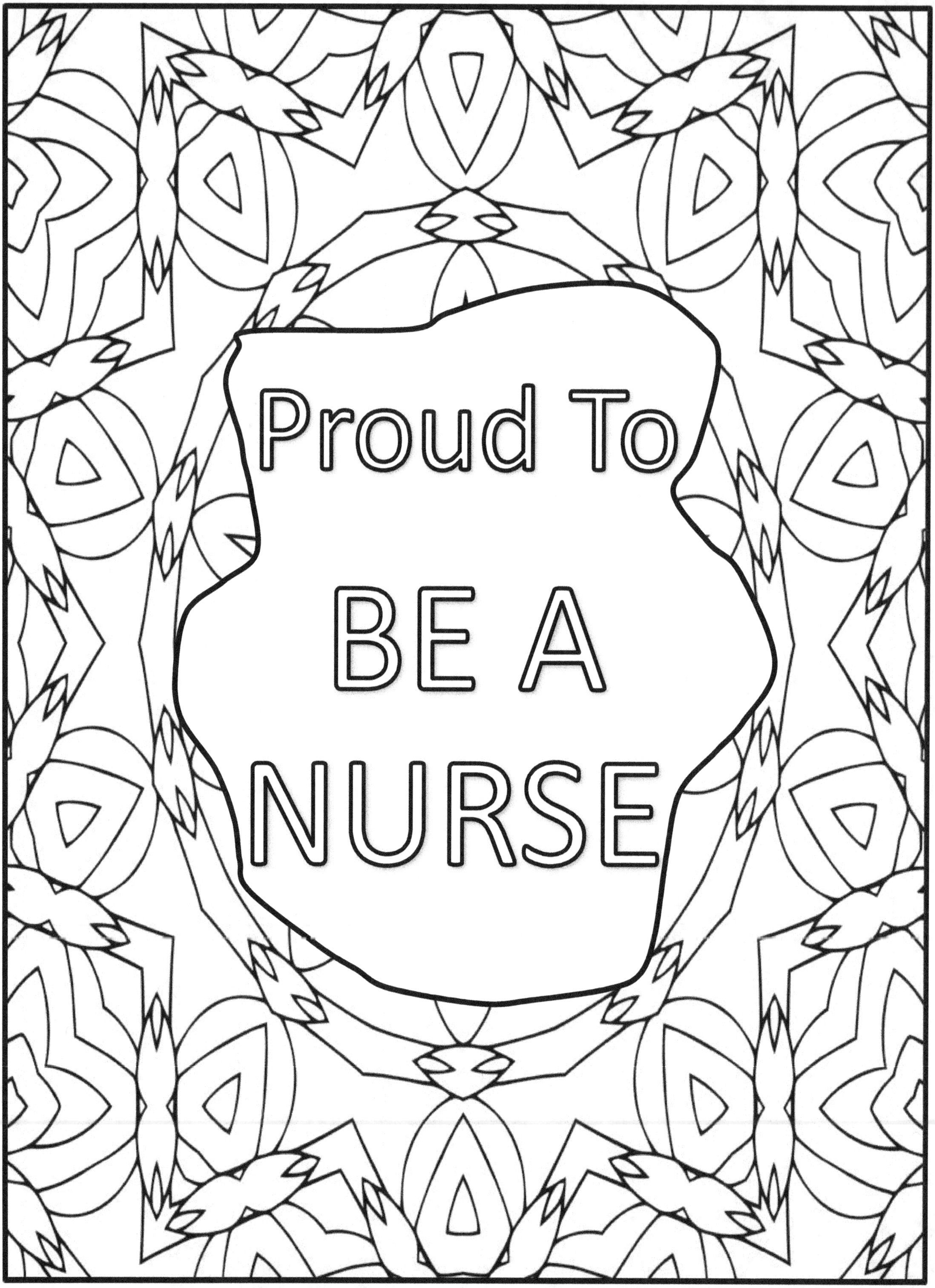
Proud To
BE A
NURSE

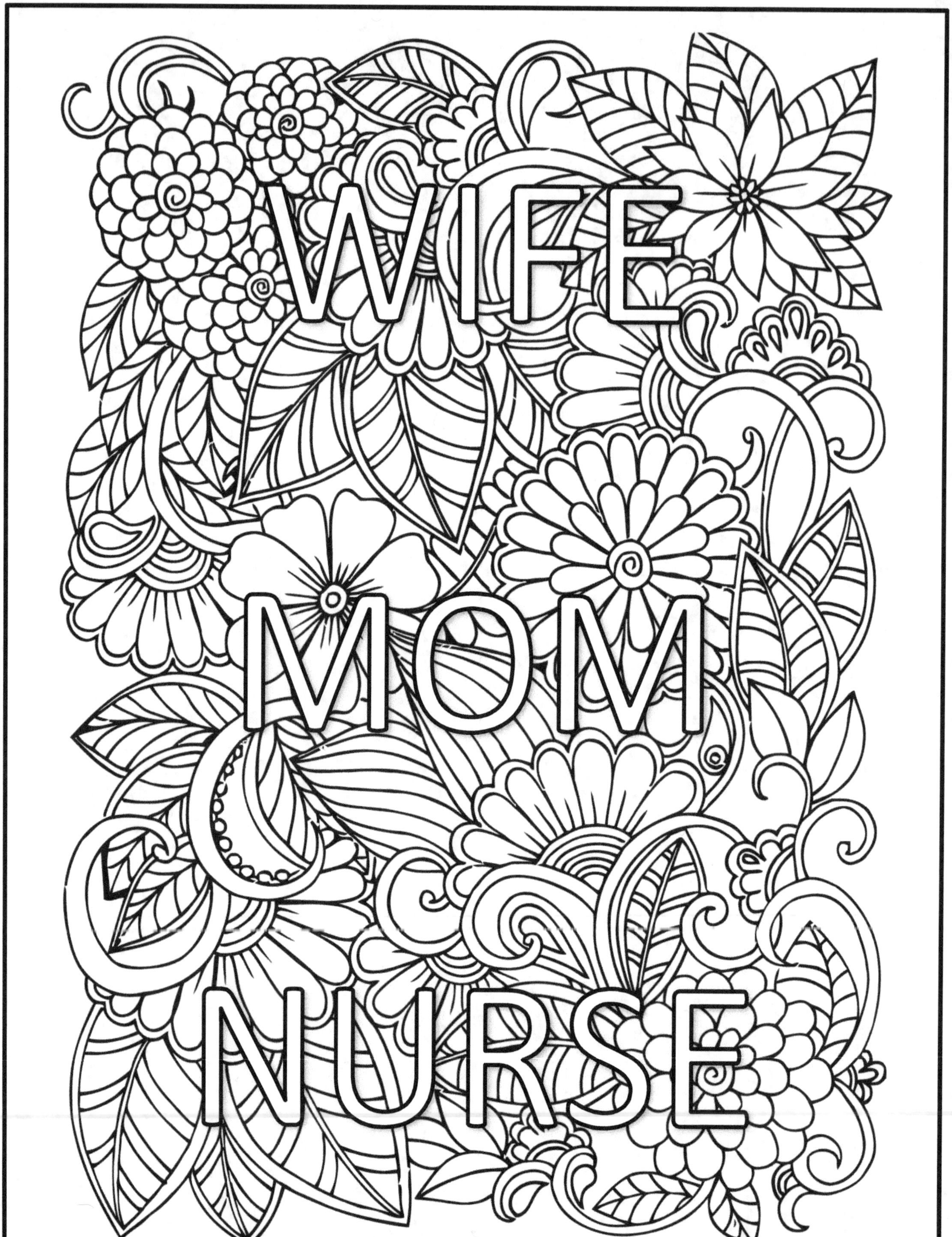
WIFE
MOM
NURSE

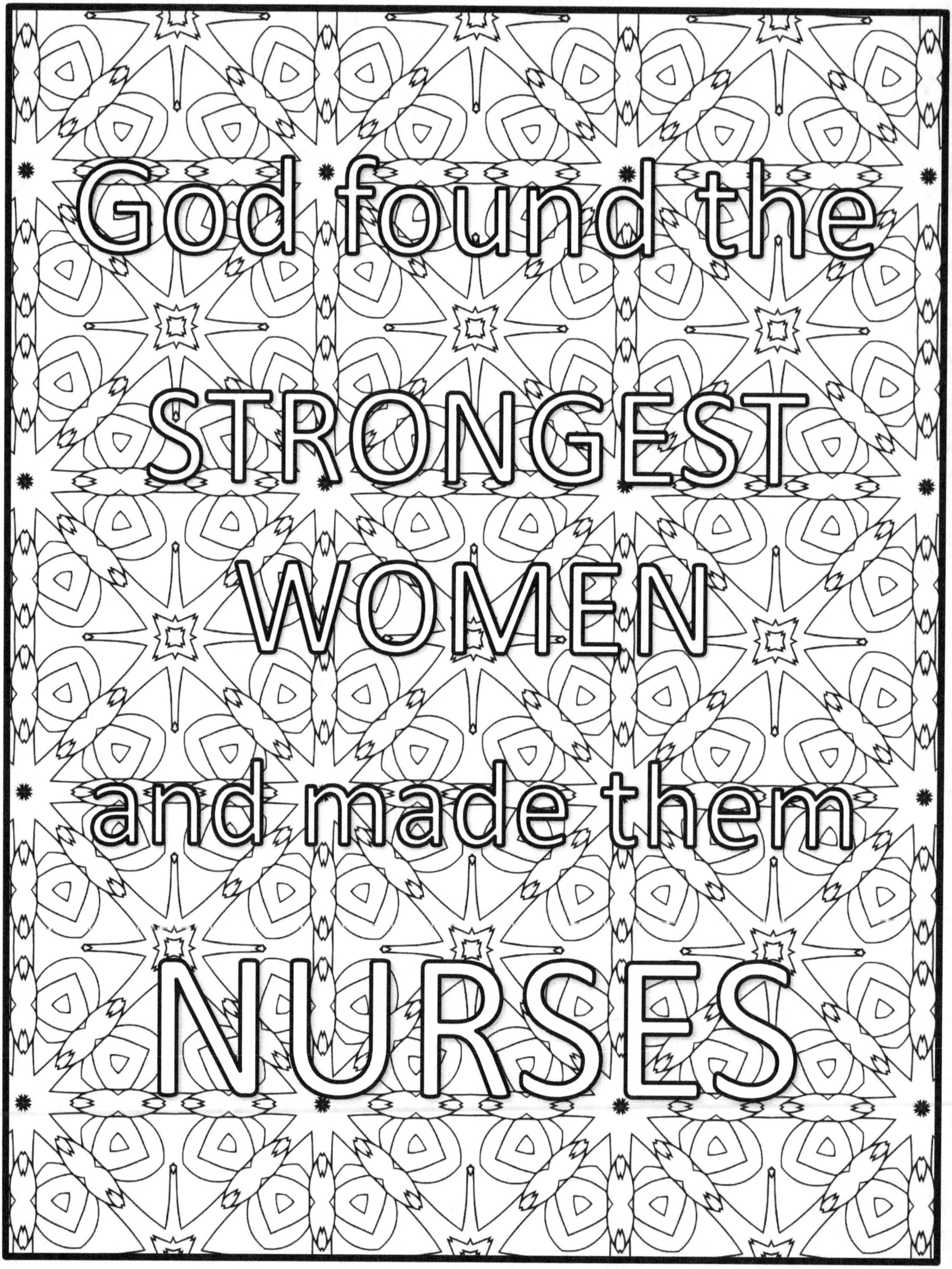
God found the
STRONGEST
WOMEN
and made them
NURSES

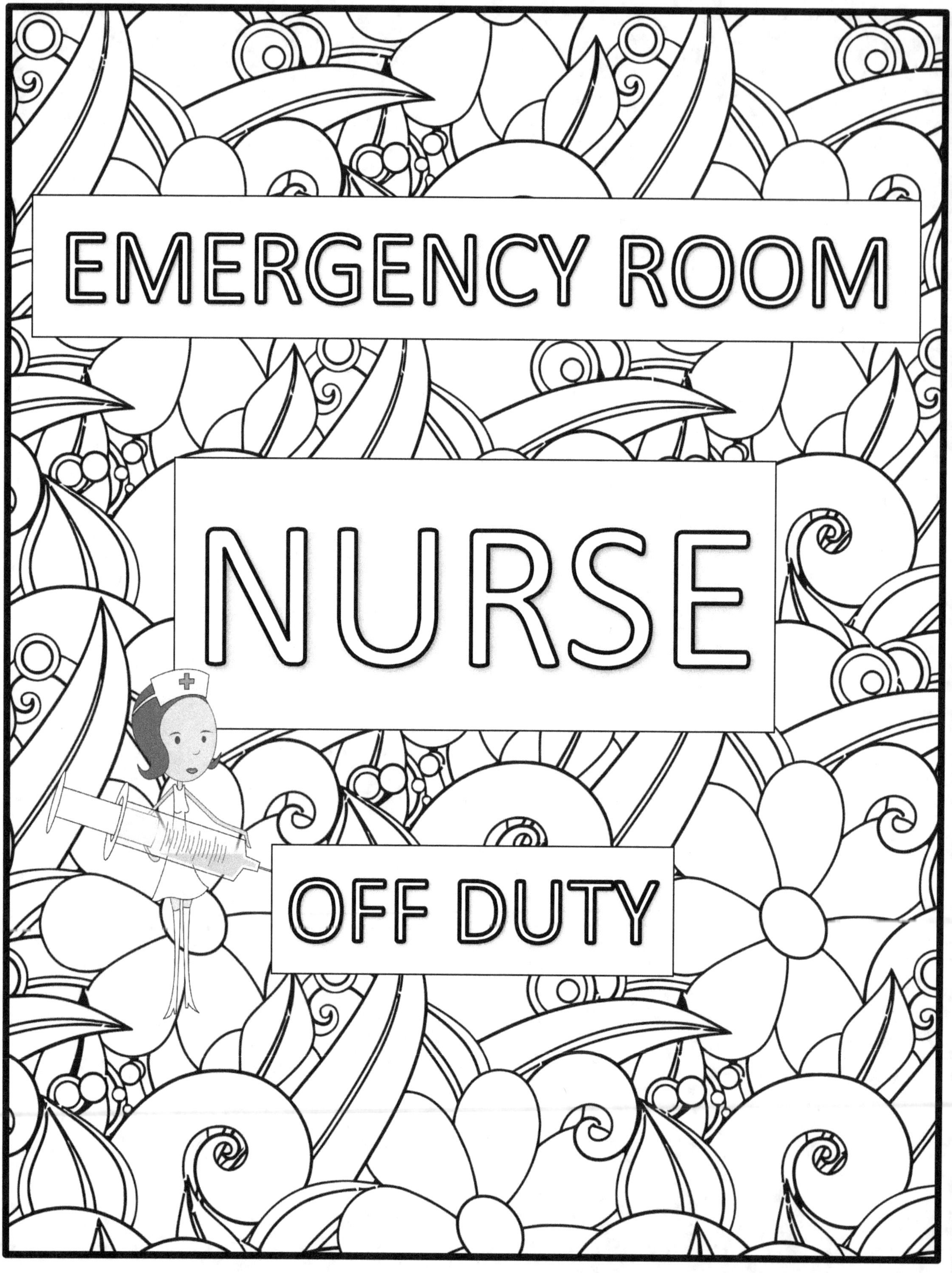
EMERGENCY ROOM
NURSE
OFF DUTY

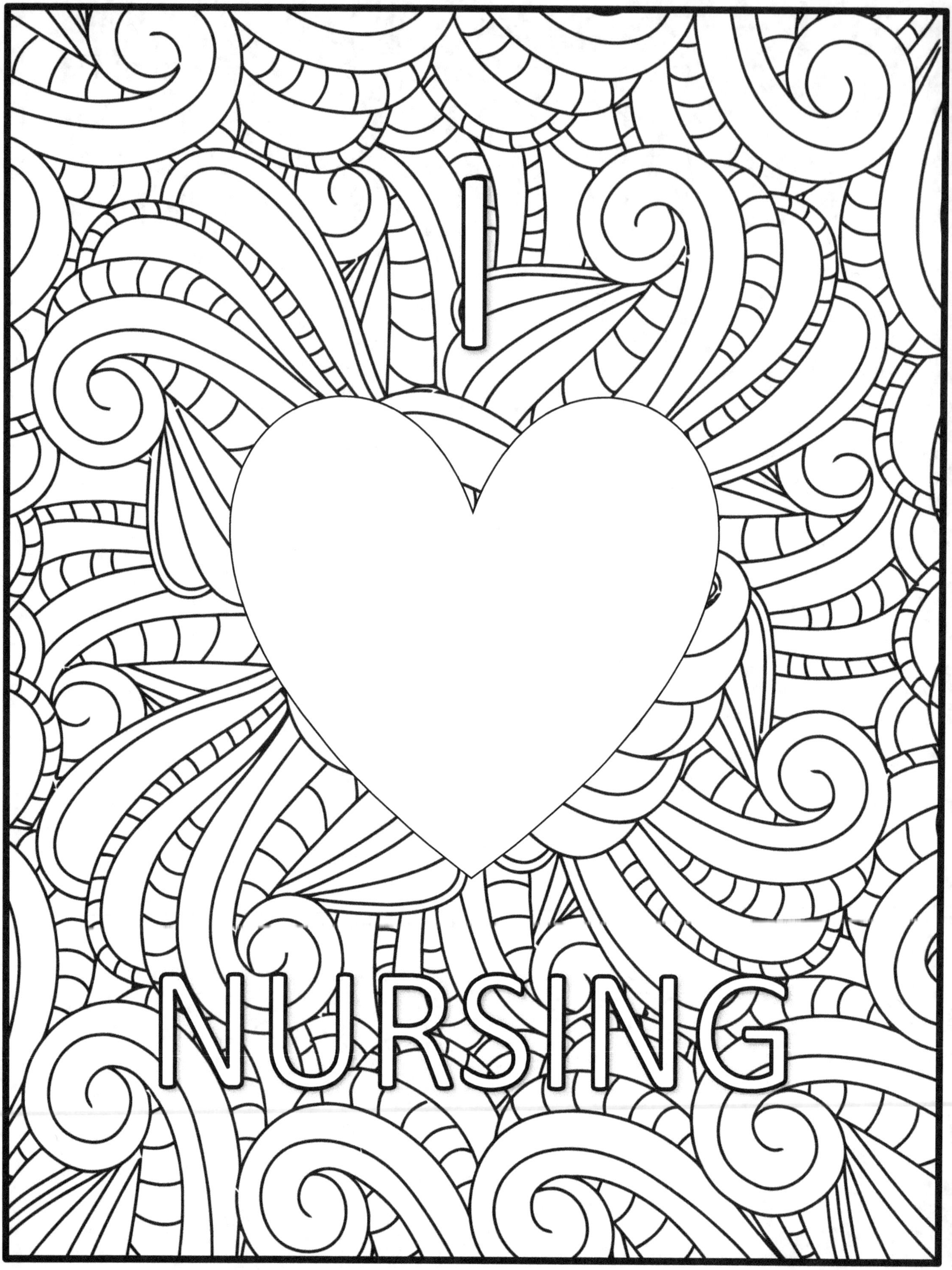
I
NURSING

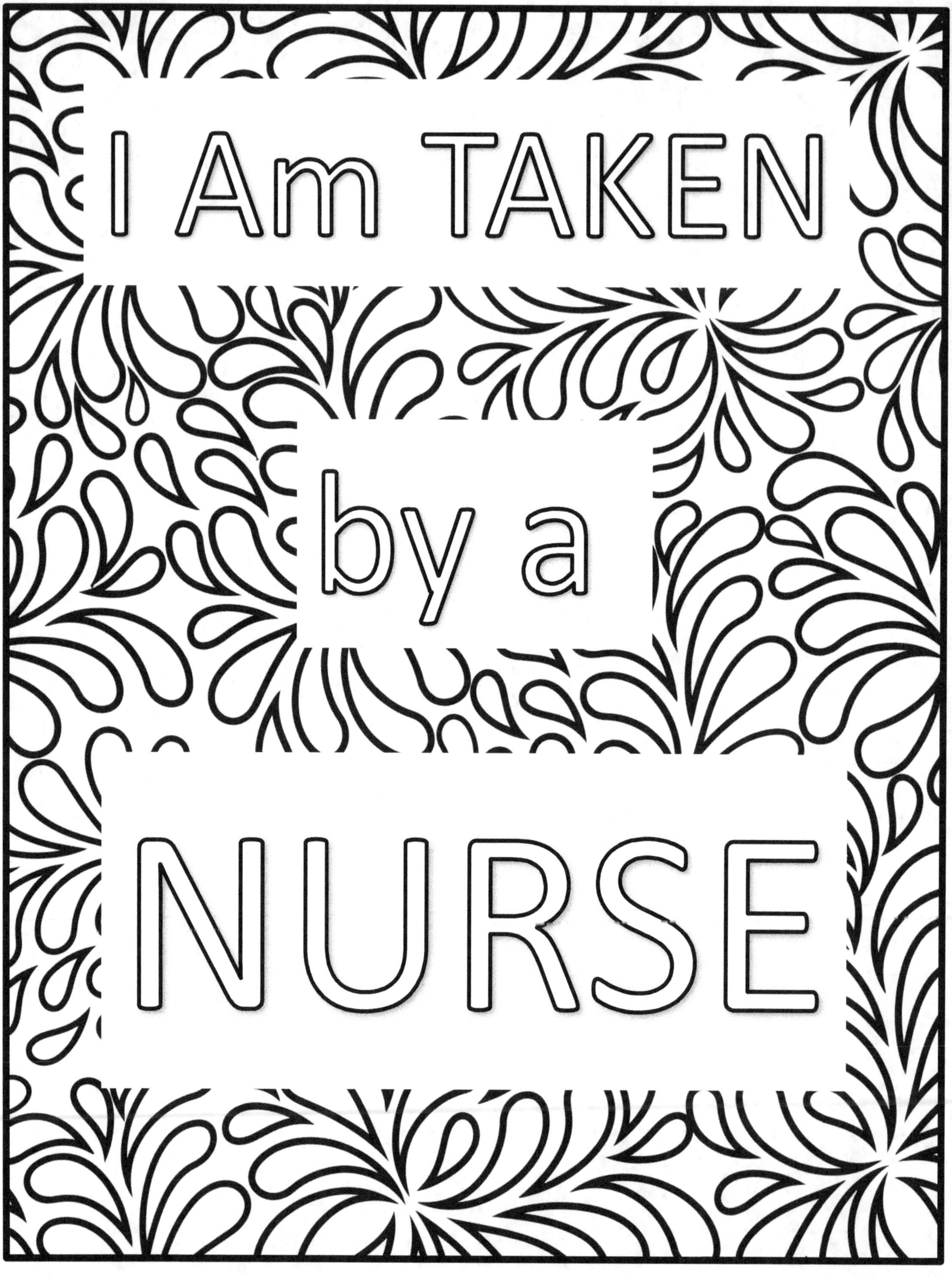
I Am TAKEN
by a
NURSE

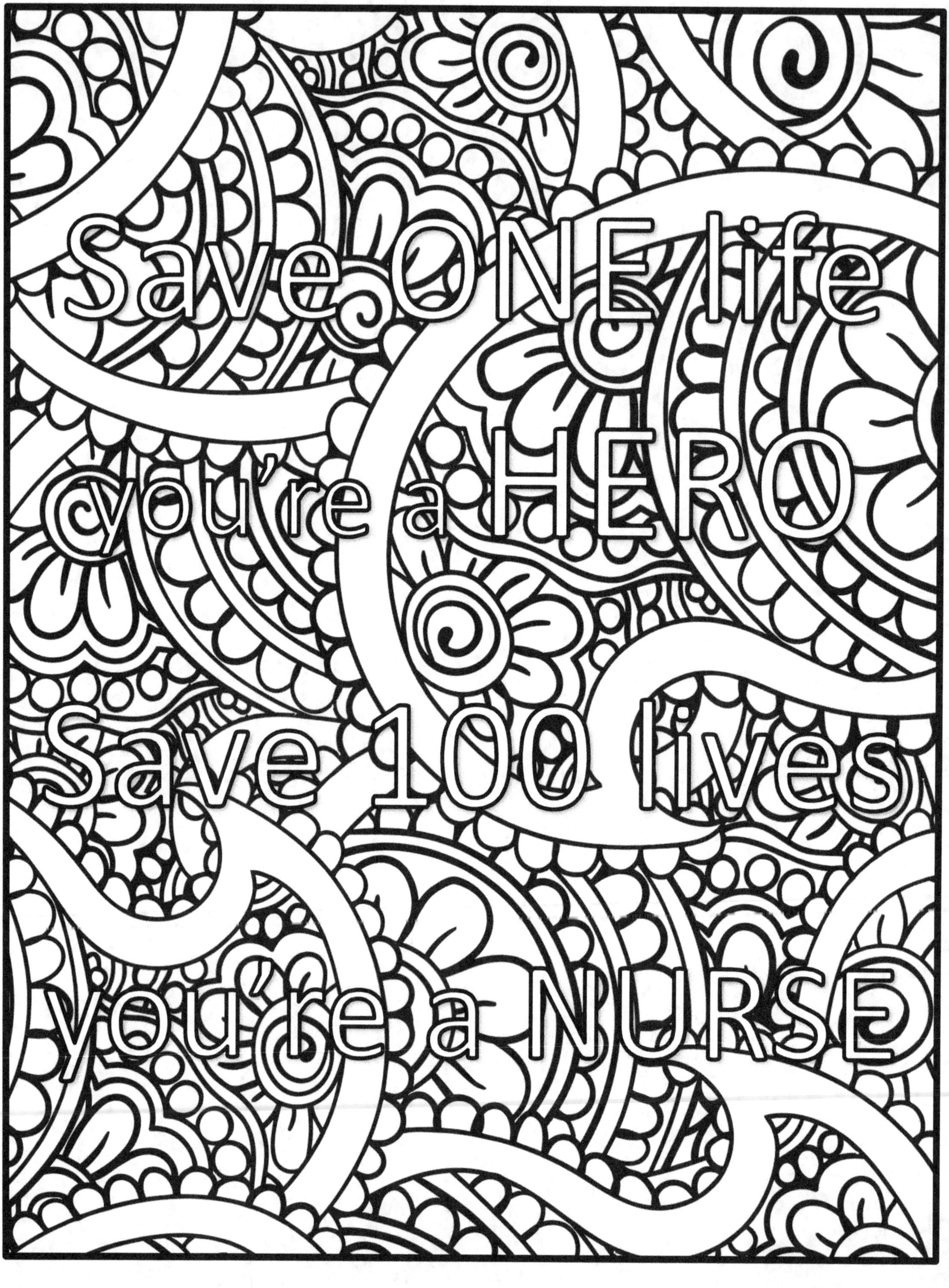
Save ONE life
you're a HERO
Save 100 lives
you're a NURSE

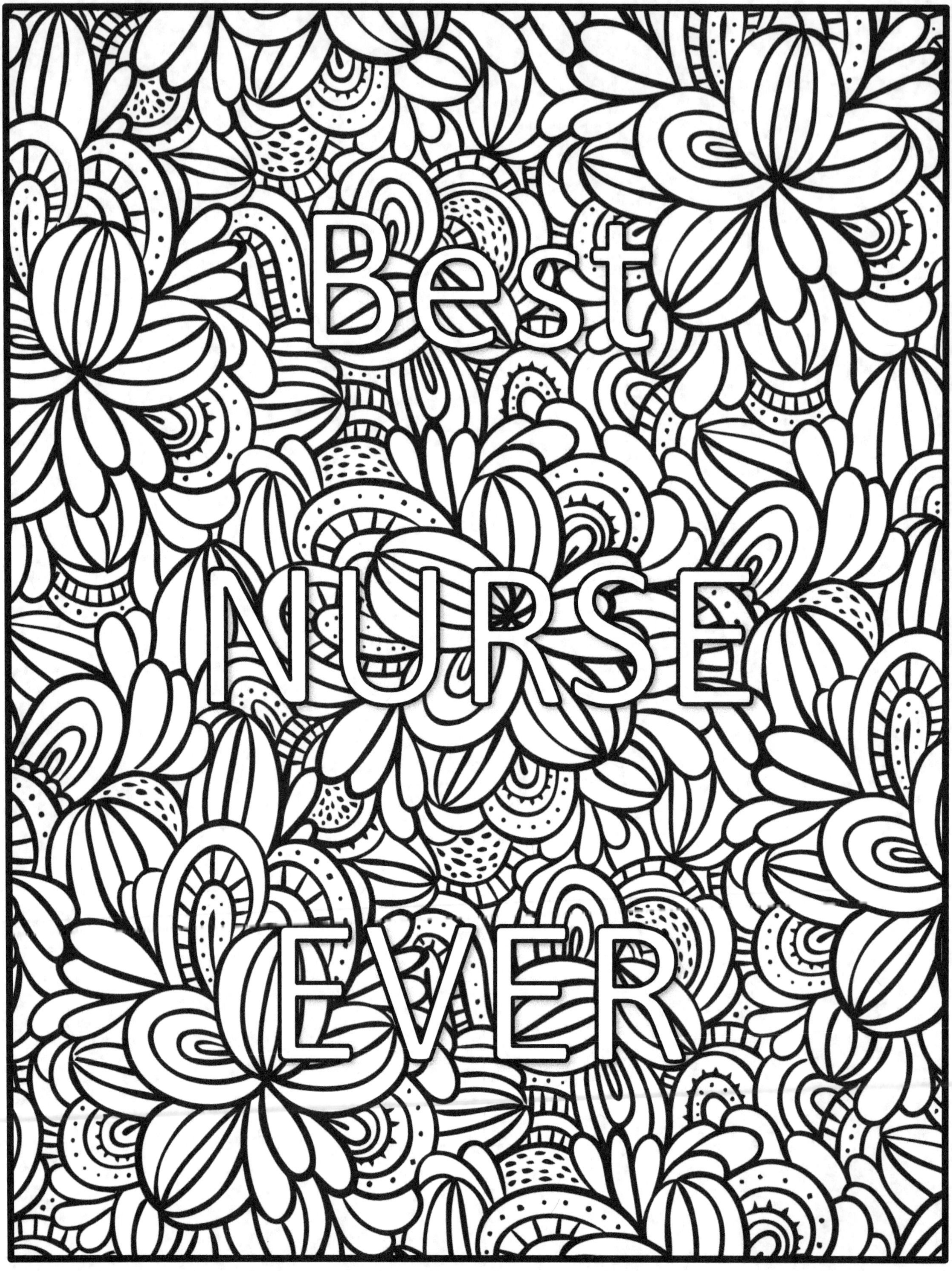
Best
NURSE
EVER

www.ingramcontent.com/pod-product-compliance
Lightning Source LLC
Chambersburg PA
CBHW081005220526
45467CB00008B/2707
9798731078801